Jesus Testifies Against The Trinity Doctrine

D.C. Dilworth

Dedication

This Book is dedicated to My Family and All People of Faith and Goodwill. In an effort to promote conscientious thought among future generations of all Believers of God's Holy Word. As written in the Bible.

Table Of Contents

Introduction.................................4

CHAPTER 1.....................................12
    Identifying The Only True God

CHAPTER 2.....................................27
    Jesus Prayed To And Worshiped
        God Our Father Only

CHAPTER 3.....................................38
    Jesus Was A Man. The Son Of Man

CHAPTER 4..................................... 52
    All Authority Given To Jesus

CHAPTER 5..................................... 60
    Beware Of False Doctrines

Appendix A...................................74
    Additional Testimony From Jesus
Refuting The Trinity

Jesus Testifies Against TheTrinity Doctrine

Introduction

In the following Research of Scripture from the Bible. The Author emphasizes the "Red-Letter" direct testimony from Jesus Himself. This will provide irrefutable evidence that the Christian Trinity, is a non-scriptural, unsubstantiated doctrine, in which most professing Christians believe. Jesus' "Red-Letter" testimony is given preeminence and frequently cited to prove this point. Along with references of Scripture from the

Apostles and Prophets. That will facilitate proof of scripture, which verifies who "the only true God" of the Bible actually is, John 17:3. The Reader will find unquestionable scriptural documentation that overwhelmingly proves. God is not a Trinity or Triune.

Jesus while praying to God. Testifies the Father "only", is the "true God" of Israel, "Father, the hour has come. Glorify Your Son,...And this is eternal life, that they may know You, the only true God" John 17:1-3. Most followers of Jesus Christ (Christians), believe He is God. Which directly contradicts Jesus' previous testimony. They believe the One God of the Bible to be a God composed of three co-equal

Persons. God the Father, God the Son (Jesus), and God the Holy Spirit. They define this non-scriptural God a Trinity, calling it a Mystery. Most Christian Scholars readily admit the word Trinity is totally absent from the pages of Scripture. Neither is there a concept of God being composed of three co-equal Persons. To the contrary, you will find that Jesus' direct testimony refutes and invalidates the claims of the Trinity doctrine, He testifies "For it is written, You shall worship the LORD your God, and Him only, you shall serve" (Matthew 4:10). "You worship what You do not know, we know what we worship, for salvation is of the Jews. But the hour is coming, and now is, when the true worshipers will worship the Father in spirit and truth, for the Father is seeking such to worship Him. God is Spirit, and those who worship Him must worship in spirit and truth" John 4:22-24. From the previous scriptures, Jesus testifies "true worshipers" should worship the "Father" as "the only true God".

Additionally, in opposition to the Trinity. Jesus teaches us that He has a God. The Father is His God, and also Our God, "I am ascending to My Father and your Father, and to My God and your God" John 20:17. "My God, My God, why have You forsaken Me ?" Matthew 27:46. Jesus also declares He's separate and unequal with His God and Father, "My Father is greater than I" John 14:28. "My Father, who has given them to Me, is greater than all" John 10:29. "Why do you call Me good ? No one is good but One, that is, God" Mark 10:18. Jesus' testimony conclusively demonstrates that God Our Father alone. Is "the only true God".

The Apostle Paul, who's credited with writing Thirteen Books in the New Testament, is of the same opinion as Jesus, "yet for us there is one God, the Father, of whom are all things" 1 Corinthians 8:6. Also, "one God and Father of all, who is above all, and through all, and in you all" Ephesians 4:6. In addition, Paul reminds Believers "All Scripture is given by inspiration of God, and is profitable for doctrine, for reproof, for correction, for instruction in righteousness, that the man of God may be complete" 2 Timothy 3:16. "Be diligent to present yourself approved to God, a worker who does not need to be ashamed, rightly dividing the word of truth" 2 Timothy 2:15. Jesus also cautions Believers to be vigilant in their Christian development to prevent being deceived, "For false christ and false prophets will rise and show great signs and wonders to deceive, if possible, even the elect" Matthew 24:24.

The above referenced testimony undeniably disproves the claims of the Trinity doctrine. Simply, the God Jesus, the Apostles and Prophets worshiped and prayed to is not a Trinity. Our Heavenly Father alone, is "the only true God". The God of Israel is not a Mystery, as most Trinitarians teach.

The Author's intention is not to criticize, defame, or vilify any particular Person or Denomination. This work comprises five Chapter Essay's, that reveal the Trinity Doctrine to be Scripturally unsupported. The Author lets the testimony of Jesus and Scripture solely interpret the subject matter. You can't find a more qualified witness than Jesus, along with the Scriptures. Who can attest to the true identity of the God of the Bible. This Research advises the Reader to use any "Red-Letter" Edition Bible. To assist in verifying the accuracy of the reference material cited. The Author utilizes the New

King James Version Bible (NKJV). Unless otherwise noted.

CHAPTER 1

Identifying The Only True God

"My Father, who has given them to Me is greater than all" John 10:29.

My Father is greater than I" John 14:28.

The idea or concept of God being composed of three co-equal Persons. Defies and opposes sound biblical scholarship. The Trinity doctrine directly contradicts both the Old and New Testament Scriptures regarding the identity of the God of Israel. Jesus throughout the Scriptures, testifies He's not the God of Israel, "My Father is greater than I" John 14:28. "Why do You call Me good ? No one is good but One, that is God" Luke 18:19. "My Father, who has given them to Me is greater than all" John 10:29. "Father,...this is eternal life, that they may know You, the only true God" John 17:1-3. "My doctrine is not Mine, but His who sent Me" John 7:16. "And the Father Himself, who sent Me, has testified of Me. You have neither heard His voice at any time, nor seen His form." John 5:37. "If I honor Myself, My honor is nothing. It is My Father who honors Me, of whom you say that He is your God" John 8:54. "For I have not spoken on My own authority, but the Father who sent Me gave Me a command, what I should say and what I should speak…Therefore, whatever I speak, just as the Father has told Me, so I speak" John 12:49-50. "I do nothing of Myself, but as My Father taught Me, I speak these things…for I always do those things that please Him" John 8:28-29.

As you can clearly see from Jesus' testimony. God is not three Persons but One. Jesus is not co-equal, but subordinate to God Our Father. As a result, the claims of the Trinity are not supported by the Scriptures.

Jesus was a Jewish Rabbi/Teacher, "Rabbi, we know that You are a teacher come from God, for no one can do these signs that You do unless God is with him" John 3:2. Jesus as a Teacher, taught what is considered the Most Important Commandment of God.

Scripture testifies, "Then one of the scribes came…asked Him, Which is the first commandment of all ? Jesus answered him, The first of all the commandments is: Hear, O Israel, the LORD our God, the LORD is one…So the scribe said to Him, Well said, Teacher. You have spoken the truth, for there is one God, and there is no other but He…Now when Jesus saw that He answered wisely, He said to him, "You are not far from the kingdom of God" Mark 12:28-34. You will find this same quote taught by Jesus. Taught by Moses, "Hear, O Israel: The LORD our God, the LORD is one !" Deuteronomy 6:4. This quote by Jesus and Moses is called the SHEMA. Which means Hear or Listen Up (Pay Attention). Many

Disciples of Judaism today, quote this phrase of Scripture twice daily. And it still is considered the Most Important Commandment. Believers must know and accept the fact that the God of Israel is One, alone. The first of God's Ten Commandments conveys this fact, "I am the LORD your God,…You shall have no other gods before Me" Exodus 20:1-3. Additionally, "I am the LORD, and there is no other, There is no God besides Me" Isaiah 45:5. "Before Me there was no God formed, Nor shall there be after Me" Isaiah 43:10. "You alone are God" Psalm 86:10. "But now, O LORD, You are our Father" Isaiah 64:8. The Scriptures are clear, the God of Israel is One alone. Never

God in three Persons, as the Trinity claims.

The true God of the Bible is referred to by different names. As we study God's Word. Utilizing accurate context is key to achieving a correct understanding of scriptures. Jesus declares, "I am the Son of God" John 10:36. Due to this declaration, various members of the Jewish Nation wanted to stone Him. Accusing Him of blasphemy. Jesus reminded them of the Authority of Jewish Law. Servants of God who genuinely receive His Word are called "gods". Jesus testifies, "Is it not written in Your law, I said, You are god's ? If He called them gods, to whom the word of God came (and the Scripture cannot be broken)" John

10:31-36. Jesus was possibly referring to Psalm 82. In which God presides over men whom He has given authority to rule and judge His people. He refers to them as "gods", counseling them to judge rightly, "God stands in the congregation of the mighty, He judges among the gods. How long will you judge unjustly. And show partiality to the wicked ?...I said You are gods, And all of you are children of the Most High. But you shall die like men, And fall like one of the princes" Psalm 82:1-8.

Following are Bible verses that identify some men as God's/god's, (lesser gods):

1. King David prophesied Jesus as His God. Psalm 45:6-7.

2. Moses was made a God to Pharaoh, Exodus 7:1.

3. Paul and Barnabas are called "gods". Acts 12:21-23.

4. Herod is called a God. Acts 12:21-23.

5. Idols are worshiped by gods. Psalm 97:7.

6. Satan is the god of this world. 2 Corinthians 4:4.

The Apostle Paul demonstrates just how critical having accurate context of scripture truly is. He cautions Believers, "For even if there are so-called gods, whether in heaven or on earth (as there are many gods and many lords), yet for us there is one God, the Father, of whom are all things" 1 Corinthians 8:5-6. King David also states, "The LORD said to my Lord, Sit at my right hand, Till I make Your enemies Your footstool" Psalm 110:1. In this verse, notice how the first spelling of LORD is all capital or uppercase letters. This identifies the true God, Our Heavenly Father. While the second spelling Lord is not all capital, but lowercase letters. Identifying a lesser God. In this case the Messiah/Christ. These are only two examples demonstrating the need for accurate context. To avoid error in understanding scripture. Following are some of the different **names and titles that identify the true God of Israel** in the Bible:

    1."**LORD**"- When all uppercase letters are used.

2."**YHWH**"- (Tetragrammaton) are   these four letters that identify "**Yaweh**"/"**Jehovah**".

3."**Yaweh**"/"**Jehovah**"-   God's Hebrew name.

4.**"Most High God"** or **"Lord God"**.

5."**Almighty**", "**God Almighty**" or "**Almighty God**".

6."**God the Father**", or just "**Father**", depending on the context.

7."Lord". This lowercase spelling strictly   depends   upon   context. Sometimes it's the true God , as in "**Lord God**", "**Lord Our God**" or "**Lord God Almighty**". Oftentimes it designates a lesser Being   .   One   who   is   in authority similar to a King, Ruler, or Master.

Jesus is Our Lord (King, Ruler, Master) . He testifies "You call Me Teacher and Lord, and you say well, for so I am" John 13:13. In addition, "All authority has been given to Me in heaven and on earth" Matthew 28:18. Also, "Father, the hour has come. Glorify Your Son…as You have given Him authority over all flesh" John 17: 1-2. Scripture also testifies, "Therefore let all the house of Israel know assuredly that God has made this Jesus whom you crucified, both Lord and Christ" Acts 2:36. Simply, God made Jesus Lord and Messiah/Christ, giving Him authority over all "in heaven and on earth". As a result, Jesus is Our Lord. Never Our God (LORD).

During Jesus Ministry, the

Jewish Nation was divided over precisely who He was. Some believed He was the Messiah/Christ. While others believed the miracles and wonders He performed were of the devil, "Therefore there was a division among the Jews…many of them said, He has a demon and is mad…Others said, These are not the words of one who has a demon. Can a demon open the eyes of the blind ?" John 10:19-21. "Therefore many from the crowd…said, Truly this is the Prophet. Others said, This is the Christ" John 7:40-44. Jesus informed them that He is the Christ and His works are the result of His relationship with God His Father, "Then the Jews surrounded Him and said to Him, How long do

You keep us in doubt ? If You are the Christ, tell us plainly. Jesus answered them, I told you, and you do not believe, The works that I do in My Fathers name, they bear witness of Me " John 10:24-25. Both God and Jesus testify that He is the Christ, "Who do men say that I, the Son of Man am?...some say John the Baptist, some Elijah…But who do you say that I am ? Simon Peter answered and said, You are the Christ, the Son of the living God…Blessed are you, Simon Bar Jonah, for flesh and blood has not revealed this to you, but My Father who is in heaven" Matthew 16:13-17. Simply, Jesus is the Son of God, Not God the Son.

The Trinity doctrine from its inception in Rome. In the year 325

AD at the First Council of Nicea. To the present date. Has created confusion and division throughout the Christian World. This is a man-made, non-scriptural doctrine, which most Christians believe is true. All true Christian worshipers must know who the Scriptures identify as the One God of Israel. To facilitate true worship to "the only true God". Jesus informs All Believers, "the true worshipers will worship the Father in spirit and truth, for the Father is seeking such to worship Him. God is Spirit, and those who worship Him must worship in spirit and truth" John 4:22-24. The true identity of God is Our Heavenly Father only !

NOTES

CHAPTER 2

Jesus Prayed To And Worshiped God Our Father Only

"In this manner, therefore, pray: **Our Father** in heaven, Hallowed be Your name…" Matthew 6:9.

"You worship what you do not know, we know what we worship, for salvation is of the Jews. But the hour is coming, and now is, when the true worshipers will worship the Father in spirit and truth, for the Father is seeking such to worship Him. God is Spirit, and those who worship Him must worship in spirit and truth" John 4:22-24.

Those who profess the God of the Bible is a Trinity. Disagree with the clear words of Jesus and

Scripture. Our worship should be acceptable to God, based on Scripture. Not on specious doctrines and traditions of men. Jesus has a God that He prays, worships and submits to. The doctrine of Jesus praying to and worshiping Himself, is totally absent from Scripture. And quite frankly illogical. Yet this is what you have to conclude, if you believe in the Trinity. With God being composed of three co-equal Persons.

Jesus prayed often to God Our Heavenly Father, "In this manner, therefore, pray: Our Father in heaven, Hallowed be Your name…" Matthew 6:9. "If you love Me, keep My commandments. And I will pray the Father, and He will give you another Helper… the Spirit of truth"

John 14:15-17. During a challenging time, prior to Jesus' arrest and crucifixion. He rebuked one of His Disciples for cutting a man's ear off. Jesus declared "Put your sword in its place,...Or do you think that I cannot now pray to My Father, and He will provide Me with more than twelve legions of angels ?" Matthew 26:53. Also in prayer, "Jesus spoke these words, lifted up His eyes to heaven, and said: Father, the hour has come. Glorify Your Son…And this is eternal life, that they may know You, the only true God" John 17:1-3. Any God other than the Father. By definition, is a False God. No God or Authority is Superior or equal to God Our Father, including Jesus, "My Father… is greater than all" John

10:29. "My Father is greater than I" John 14:28. Notice, Jesus just proclaimed the Father alone, is Supreme above all. This fact alone disproves the Trinity.

In previous verses, Jesus and Scripture have conclusively established that Jesus has a God He Prays to. And that His Father is **"the only true God"**. Jesus worships the Father as His God. After further scriptural study, let's now see who Jesus defines as "true worshipers", He testifies, "You worship, what you do not know, we know what we worship, for salvation is of the Jews. But the hour is coming and now is when the **true worshipers** will **worship the Father in spirit and truth**, for the Father is seeking such to worship

Him. God is Spirit, and those who worship Him **must worship in spirit and truth**" John 4:22-24. From the previous testimony of Jesus, one can conclude, **"true worshipers" "must worship in spirit and truth" "the only true God", "the Father"**.

It's Scripturally inaccurate to believe that the God of Israel is composed of three co-equal Persons. As proven previously, not only is God and Jesus unequal. They are also different and distinct, not sharing the same will. Jesus always submitted to His Father's will over His own, "Father if it is your will take this cup from Me, nevertheless not My will, But yours be done" Luke 22:42. "I can of Myself do nothing...I do not seek

My own will but the will of the Father who sent Me" John 5:30. "My food is to do the will of Him who sent Me, and to finish His work" John 4:34. "I do nothing of Myself, but as My Father taught Me, I speak these things…For I always do those things that please Him" John 8:28. "My doctrine is not Mine, but His who sent Me" John 7:16. Jesus never professed or inferred God to be a Trinity of Persons or Himself. He reveres and submits to His God, "My God, My God, why have You forsaken Me ?" Matthew 27:46. On four occasions in one verse. Jesus shows reverence to His God, declaring "He who overcomes, I will make him a pillar in the temple of My God and he shall go out no more. I will write on him the name of My God and the name of the city of My God, the New Jerusalem, which comes down out of heaven from My God" Revelation 3:12. **Jesus has a God** that He Prays, Worships and Submits to. The same God that all Believers should Pray, Worship and Submit to. Simply, Jesus and <u>True Worshipers</u> share in common the same God, "I am ascending to My Father and your Father, and to My God and your God" John 20:17. **Jesus' God is also Our God. The Heavenly Father Only.**

Jesus was a Jewish Rabbi/Teacher, "You call Me Teacher and Lord, and you are correct for so I am" John 13:13 (NASB). "But for you, do not be called Rabbi, for One is your

Teacher the Christ, and you are all brethren. Do not call anyone on earth your father, for One is your Father, He who is in heaven," Matthew 23:8-10. Jesus' Disciples referred to and considered Him their Teacher. Never the God of Israel. They knew the difference and distinction, "Rabbi, we know that You are a Teacher Come from God, for no one can do these signs that You do unless God is with him" John 3:2. "In the meantime His disciples urged Him, saying Rabbi eat" John 4:31. "They said to Him, Rabbi, where are You staying ?" John 1:38. Clearly, Jesus nor His Disciples believed that He was God.

Jesus testifies, He is the Son of God, "But who do you say that I, the Son of Man am ? Simon Peter answered and said, You are the Christ, the Son of the living God. Jesus answered and said to him, Blessed are you, Simon Bar-Jonah, for flesh and blood has not revealed this to you, but My Father who is in heaven" Matthew 16:13-17. God Himself confirms this declaration, "This is My beloved Son, in whom I am well pleased. Hear Him !" Matthew 17:5. Jesus is not God the Son, as most Trinitarians teach. But rather, the "Son of God" as Scripture teaches, Jesus testifies "I said, I am the Son of God" John 10:36.

As "true worshipers" of "the only true God" "Our Father in

heaven". True Believers must closely examine Scripture and are reminded to, "Study to shew thyself approved unto God, a workman that needeth not to be ashamed, rightly dividing the word of truth" 2 Timothy 2:15. Nothing in Scripture states or comes close to suggesting. That the God of the Bible, is equal to and submits to anyone or anything. Our Heavenly Father is "the only true God".

NOTES

CHAPTER 3
Jesus Was A Man. The Son Of Man.

"God is not a man that He should lie, Nor a son of man" Numbers 23:19.

"But now you seek to kill Me, a Man who has told you the truth which I heard from God" John 8:40.

By adhering to the Trinity doctrine. The majority of Christians today, continue to believe that Jesus is God. The Scriptures are absolutely clear. The God of Israel is not a Man. "I am God and not man" Hosea 11:9. "God is not a man that He should lie, Nor a son of man" Numbers 23:19. Jesus taught

His Disciples and subsequent Believers, that He was a Man, not God "But now you seek to kill Me, a Man who has told you the truth which I heard from God" John 8:40. Yes the Man Jesus has a God He submits to, "My God, My God, why have You forsaken Me ?" Matthew 27:46. Jesus' God, is Our Heavenly Father. The very same God that He has in common with all Believers, "I am ascending to My Father and your Father and to My God and your God" John 20:17. True Believers must worship only God Our Father as Jesus did. He testifies, "You worship what you do not know, we know what we worship, for salvation is of the Jews. But the hour is coming, and now is, when the true worshipers

39

will worship the Father in spirit and truth, for the Father is seeking such to worship Him. God is Spirit, and those who worship Him must worship in spirit and truth" John 4:22-24. It is scripturally inaccurate to assume the Man Jesus is worshiping Himself as God. By definition, Jesus cannot be God, since He has a God He worships.

The phrase son of man, simply means mankind. One who is of the human race, a human being. Man was made by God, lower than angels. Jesus included. The Old and New Testament Scriptures practically testify verbatim, "What is man that you are mindful of him, Or the son of man that You take care of him ? You have made him a little lower than the angels" Hebrews 2:6-7 and Psalm 8:4-5. Jesus the Son of Man (a Human), was also made "lower than the angels", "But we see Jesus, who was made a little lower than the angels" Hebrews 2:9. Nothing in scripture indicates that God was made. Let alone, made "lower than the angels" ! Since Jesus was made by God. Again, by definition, He cannot be God. The God of Israel has no beginning or ending, but is everlasting, "Before the mountains were brought forth, Or ever You had formed the earth and the world, Even from everlasting to everlasting, You are God" Psalm 90:2.

Jesus considered, and often referred to Himself as "the Son of Man", He testifies "For even the Son of Man did not come to be served, but to serve, and to give His life a ransom for many" Mark 10:45. Also, "the Son of Man has come to seek and to save that which was lost" Luke 19:10. Jesus is not just a son of man. He is "the Son of Man" foretold or prophesied by the Prophet Daniel, Jesus testifies "When the Son of Man comes in His glory, and all the angels with Him, then He will sit on the throne of His glory" Matthew 25:31. Daniel foresaw the coming of Jesus. God's Messiah/Christ, who has all authority in heaven and earth granted to Him from God. Daniel testifies, "I was watching in the night visions, And behold, One like the Son of Man, Coming with the clouds of heaven !...Then to Him was given dominion and glory and a kingdom,...His dominion is an everlasting dominion, Which shall not pass away" Daniel 7:13-14. This Prophecy by Daniel was fulfilled. As Jesus confirmed that He was the Christ, the Son of God. As a result of this declaration, Jesus was accused of blasphemy and sentenced to death. Scripture testifies, "Again the high priest asked Him, saying to Him, Are You the Christ, the Son of the Blessed ? Jesus said, I am. And you will see the Son of Man sitting at the right hand of the Power, and coming with the clouds of heaven. Then the high priest tore his clothes and said,

What further need do we have of witnesses? You have heard the blasphemy! What do you think? And they all condemned Him to be deserving of death" Mark 14:61-64. Jesus was crucified for claiming that He was "the Christ, the Son of the Blessed". Not for being the God of Israel. Scripture further testifies proving this point, "And they put up over His head the accusation written against Him: THIS IS JESUS THE KING OF THE JEWS…If You are the Son of God, come down from the cross….If He is the King of Israel, let Him come down…He trusted in God, let Him deliver Him now if He will have Him, for He said, I am the Son of God". Matthew 27:36-43.

The Scriptures are indisputable. Not only did Jesus consider Himself a Man and not God. His Disciples and the whole of Scripture confirms it. The following verses of Scripture clearly demonstrate, the attributes of God differ greatly from those of Jesus.

1."For there is one God and one Mediator between God and men, the Man, Christ Jesus" 1 Timothy 2:5.

2."For if by one man's offense many died, much more the grace of God and the gift by the grace of the one Man, Jesus Christ" Romans 5:15.

3."God…has appointed a day on which He will judge the world in righteousness by the Man whom He has ordained" Acts 17:30-31.

4. God is perfect.-"As for God, his way is perfect" Psalm 18:30.

Jesus was made perfect.-"though He was a Son, yet He learned obedience by the things which He suffered. And having been perfected, He became the author of eternal salvation to all who obey Him, called by God as High Priest" Hebrews 5:8-10.

5. God is Supreme above all, Omnipotent (all powerful).-"For the LORD God Omnipotent reigns !" Revelation 19:6. "But our God is in heaven ,He does whatever He pleases" Psalm 115:3.

Jesus is inferior to God. Not co-equal, as the Trinity doctrine teaches.-"My Father is greater than I" John 14:28. "My Father, who has given them to Me,is greater than all" John 10:29.

6. God is all knowing (Omniscient).-"God is greater than our heart, and knows all things" 1 John 3:20.

Jesus had limited knowledge.-"But of that day and hour no one knows, not even the angels in heaven, nor the Son, but only the Father" Mark 13:32. "Jesus increased in wisdom and stature, and in favor with God and men" Luke 2:52.

Jesus was a Man, certified by the God of Israel, "Men of Israel hear these words: Jesus of Nazareth, a Man attested (certified) by God to you by miracles, wonders, and signs which God did through Him in your midst, as you yourselves also know" Acts 2:22. As a result of being "a Man attested by God". Jesus was also a Man anointed with the Power of God's Holy Spirit, "God anointed Jesus of Nazareth with the Holy Spirit and with power, who went about doing good and healing all who were oppressed by the devil, for God was with Him" Acts 10:38.

From the above-mentioned verses of Scripture. One must conclude that Jesus is not God. No verse of Scripture testifies that the God of Israel is three-Persons. To the contrary, Jesus states that the Father is "the only true God" John 17:1-3. Simply, Jesus was a Man made by God. God was not made, but is from "everlasting to everlasting". Having no beginning or ending.

So who do you believe ? The clear words of Jesus and Scripture ? Or the non-scriptural, man-made doctrine of the Trinity ? The definition of Idolatry is worshiping and believing as God. A God who is not God. Jesus testifies who God actually is,"Father, the hour has come. Glory Your Son,...And this is eternal life, that they may know You, the only true God". True Believers must ,"Study to shew thyself approved unto God, a workman that needeth not to be ashamed, rightly dividing the word of truth" 2 Timothy 2:15, (KJV). Our Heavenly Father Alone. Is the True God of the Bible !

NOTES

CHAPTER 4

All Authority Given To Jesus

"All authority has been given to Me in heaven and on earth" Matthew 28:18.

"All things have been delivered to Me by My Father" Matthew 11:27.

When it comes to learning what is true regarding the Bible. Believers in Jesus must be diligent to closely examine His words along with what the whole of Scripture states. Making sure to trust, but also to actually verify the teaching. Jesus has been granted all authority by God Our Heavenly Father. Although His authority is given to Him. It is not absolute authority. Absolute total authority is reserved only for God alone. In the following testimony from Jesus and Scripture. Evidence will conclusively provide proof that Jesus' authority is subordinate to and originates from God. Our Heavenly Father's authority reigns Supreme above all. Including Jesus.

Jesus testifies, "All things have been delivered to Me by My Father" Matthew 11:27. "For I have not spoken on My own authority, but the Father who sent Me gave Me a command, what I should say and what I should speak…Therefore, whatever I speak, just as the Father has told Me, so I speak" John 12:49-50. "All authority has been given to Me in heaven and on earth" Matthew 28:18. "Father, the hour has come. Glorify Your Son, that Your Son may glorify You, as You have given him authority over all flesh" John 17:1-2. Jesus is also entrusted and permitted to carry out "all judgment", testifying "For the Father judges no one, but has committed all judgment to the Son" John 5:22. "For as the Father has life in Himself, so He has granted the Son to have life in Himself, and has given Him authority to execute judgment" John 5:26-27.

God's authority is completely and totally absolute. Jesus is subordinate to God, doing His Father's will and speaking His Father's words, "I can of Myself do nothing. As I hear, I judge, and My judgment is righteous, because I do not seek My own will but the will of the Father who sent Me" John 5:30. "The words that I speak to you I do not speak on My own authority, but the Father who dwells in Me does the works" John 14:10. "I do nothing of Myself, but as My Father taught Me, I speak these things…The Father has not left Me alone, for I always do those things that please Him" John 8:28-29. Scripture corroborates and validates Jesus testimony, "For He whom God has sent speaks the words of God, for God does not give the Spirit by measure. The Father loves the Son, and has given all things into His hand" John 3:34-35.

Although Jesus has all authority in heaven and earth. It must be noted that God is excluded. Scripture teaches Jesus will conquer all authority, power and rule to deliver "the kingdom to God the Father...The last enemy to be destroyed is death" 1 Corinthians 15:24-26. Then all things will be brought under Jesus' feet. Except for God Himself. The Apostle Paul states it this way, "But when He says, all things are put under Him, it is evident that He who put all things under Him is excepted. Now when all things are made subject to Him, the Son Himself will also be subject to Him, who put all things under Him, that God may be all in all" 1 Corinthians 15:24-28. Paul just expressed that Jesus is subordinate and subject to God's Supreme authority everlastingly ("all in all"). Paul further testifies, "the head of

Christ is God". 1 Corinthians 11:3. Additionally, He states, "For even if there are so-called gods, whether in heaven or on earth (as there are many gods and many lords), yet for us there is one God, the Father, of whom are all things" 1 Corinthians 8:5-6. We are also reminded by Jesus of God's total and complete authority, "My Father is greater than I" and "My Father...is greater than all".

In the preceding testimony from Jesus and Scripture. God's Authority is complete, total and absolute. All Jesus' authority was given to Him, deriving from God. As a result, the claim of the Trinity doctrine, that the God of the Bible is three-Persons and co-equal with Jesus. Has no basis in fact from the

Scriptures. Without question, Our Heavenly Father alone is "the only true God", according to Jesus and the Scriptures.

NOTES

CHAPTER 5

Beware Of False Doctrines

"And in vain they worship Me, Teaching as doctrines the commandments of men" Mark 7:7.

"Beware of false prophets, who come to you in sheep's clothing, but inwardly they are ravenous wolves" Matthew 7:15.

The Doctrines of a particular Denomination or Church, are the teachings that govern its beliefs. Consequently, having sound doctrine is the fundamental basis of one's faith. That's why it's of major importance, to make sure the doctrine Believers follow, aligns with Scripture, "All Scripture is given by inspiration of God, and is profitable for doctrine, for reproof, for correction, for instruction in righteousness, that the man of God may be complete" 2 Timothy 3:16. Also, "For the time will come when they will not tolerate sound doctrine…and they will turn their ears away from the truth and will turn aside to myths" 2 Timothy 4:3-4. Modern Christian Scholarship readily admits. The Trinity doctrine is a mystery/myth. The doctrinal concept of one God in three-Persons, as most Trinitarians teach. Is completely absent from Scripture. Scripture consistently teaches, the God of Israel is One, alone.

The mistaken belief that God is a Trinity. Is the most influential doctrine adversely affecting Christians faith today. Jesus testifies He is not God. God is truly only the Father, "Father,...this is eternal life that they may know You, the only true God" John 17:1-3. Jesus also testifies, the most important Commandment is to know and believe the doctrine, that the God of Israel is One,"The first of all the commandments is: Hear O Israel, the LORD our God, the LORD is one" Mark 12:29. Jesus also declares "This people honors Me with their lips, But their heart is far from Me. And in vain do they worship Me , Teaching as doctrines the commandments of men. For laying aside the commandment of God, you hold the tradition of men...All too well you reject the commandment of God, that you may keep your tradition" Mark 7:6-9. The Apostle Paul concurs that God is one, the Father only, "yet for us there is one God, the Father" 1 Corinthians 8:6. Also, "one God and Father of all, who is above all" Ephesians 4:6. Old Testament Prophets agree as well, "Have we not all one Father ? Has not one God created us ?" Malachi 2:10. "You alone are God" Psalm 86:10. The Scriptures are unquestionably clear. God is One, alone. Never three, as the Trinity doctrine represents.

Jesus instructs Believers to choose the narrow door. Which many will not find. And to "Beware of false Prophets" who pretend to know the way to eternal life, yet their path "leads to destruction", Jesus testifies "Enter by the narrow gate, for wide is the gate and broad is the way that leads to destruction, and there are many who go in by it. Because narrow is the gate and difficult is the way which leads to life, and there are few who find it. Beware of false prophets, who come to you in sheep's clothing, but inwardly they are ravenous wolves" Matthew 7:13-15. Diligent Believers will be able to detect false teachers, by observing their actions, "You will know them by their fruit", Matthew 7:16. How they actually conduct their lives. Making sure their words and deeds align with Scripture, "For false christs and false prophets will rise and show great signs and wonders to deceive, if possible even the elect" Matthew 24:24.

Jesus further instructs Believers. To do God's will and adhere to sound doctrines, aligning with Scripture. To avoid being deceived. Keeping in mind, we must do/perform those precepts taught in Scripture, "Not everyone who says to Me Lord, Lord, shall enter the kingdom of heaven, but he who does the will of My Father in heaven. Many will say to Me in that day, Lord, Lord, have we not prophesied in Your name, cast out demons in Your name, and done many wonders in your name ? And then I will declare to them, I never knew you, depart from Me, you who practice lawlessness !" Matthew 7:21-23. "But why do you call Me

Lord, Lord, and not do the things which I say?" Luke 6:46. The consequences of believing non-scriptural doctrines and traditions, is that many will be deceived. Falsely believing they merit eternal life. But Jesus may announce to them, "I never knew you, depart from Me".

James, the brother of Jesus also reminds Believers, "Be doers of the word, and not hearers only, deceiving yourselves" James 1:22. In addition, "faith by itself, if it does not have works, is dead. But someone will say, You have faith, and I have works. Show me your faith without your works, and I will show you my faith by my works" James 2:17-18. "You see then that a man is justified by works and not by faith only…For as the body without the spirit is dead, so faith without works is dead also" James 2:24-26.

Jesus Disciples also cautions Believers to examine doctrines carefully, to make certain they coincide with the Bible. The Apostle John warns of deceptive, antichrist teachers, "For many deceivers have gone out into the world who do not confess Jesus Christ as coming in the flesh, (as a Man). This is a deceiver and antichrist" 2 John 1:7. Scripture teaches "God is not a man" Numbers 23:19. Therefore Jesus cannot be God, since He was a Man, "But now you seek to kill Me, a Man who has told you the truth which I heard from God" John 8:40. John continues, "Whoever transgresses and does not abide in the doctrine of Christ does not have God. He who abides in the doctrine of Christ has both the Father and Son. If anyone comes to you and does not bring this doctrine, do not receive him" 2 John 1:9. Under close examination of the Trinity. You will find that it definitely "transgresses and does not abide in the doctrine of Christ", Jesus taught "My Father is greater than I" John 14:28. "My Father… is greater than all" John 10:29. "Why do you call Me good ? No one is good but One, that is God" Mark 10:18. "I can of Myself do nothing" John 5:30. "My doctrine is not Mine, But His who sent Me" John 7:16. These are only a few of the doctrines that Jesus taught, which clearly demonstrate that he is not co-equal or part of a three-Person God. True Believers must carefully study what Jesus actually taught. To authenticate that the words of Ministers and Teachers are in accordance with Scripture.

The Apostle Paul cautions Believers that there would be those who turn away (apostasy) from the true faith of Christ. To seek after "doctrines of demons" filled with lies and deceit. Paul testifies, "Now the Spirit expressly says that in latter times some will depart from the faith, giving heed to deceiving spirits and doctrines of demons, speaking lies in hypocrisy" 1 Timothy 4:1-2. "Be diligent to present yourself approved to God, a worker who does not need to be ashamed, rightly dividing the word of truth" 2 Timothy 2:15. Paul also teaches, "we should no longer be children, tossed to and fro and carried about with every wind of doctrine, by the trickery of men, in the cunning craftiness of deceitful plotting" Ephesians 4:14.

The Apostle Peter, forewarns against false prophets that will be among the faithful. Deceiving many with destructive doctrines that turn truth into deception, "But there were also false prophets among the people, even as there will be false teachers among you, who will secretly bring in destructive heresies…And many will follow their destructive ways, because of whom the way of truth will be blasphemed. By covetousness they will exploit you with deceptive words" 2 Peter 2:1-3.

True Believers must differentiate between false and true doctrine. True doctrine comes from Scripture. The inspired Words of God, as written throughout the Bible. Those who listen, obey, and follow Jesus' example, are worthy to enter the Kingdom, "Most assuredly, I say to you, if anyone keeps My word he shall never see death" John 8:51. Scripture affords Believers a final warning. Don't deviate from Doctrine found in Scripture ! "For I testify to everyone who hears the words of the prophecy of this book: If anyone adds to these things, God will add to Him the plagues that are written in this book, and if anyone takes away from the words of the book of this prophecy, God shall take away his part from the Book of Life." Revelation 22:18-19. God Our Heavenly Father Alone Is, "the only true God" !

P.S.- If You found this Book beneficial. Please share a copy with other Believers and write a Review on Amazon. Thank You, God Bless.

About The Author

D.C.Dilworth is a Sunday school Bible study teacher. Who is an avid lifelong passionate student of biblical truth, as written within the Holy Scriptures of the Bible. This passion to comprehend and exam scripture, has led me to conclusions that challenge traditional beliefs as to who the God of the Bible actually is.

As a result of diligent, meticulous research of scripture. I found myself questioning the validity of church beliefs concerning the doctrine of the Trinity. Simply, the God of the Bible whom Jesus, the Apostles and Prophets prayed to and worshiped is not a Trinity.

Throughout this book I share Jesus'" Red Letter" testimony. Along with scripture from the Apostles and Prophets that disproves without question, the claims of theTrinity doctrine. As the Author, my intention is not to criticize, defame or vilify any person or denomination. I let the testimony of Jesus and scripture to serve as the most authoritative source to identify the true identity of the God of the Bible.

NOTES

APPENDIX A

Additional Testimony From Jesus Refuting The Trinity

1. "And the Father Himself, who sent Me, has testified of Me. You have neither heard His voice at any time, nor seen His form" John 5:37.

2. "If you love Me, keep My commandments. And I will pray the Father, and He will give you another Helper…the Spirit of truth" John 14:15-17.

3. "But the Helper, the Holy Spirit, whom the Father will send in My name, He will teach you all things" John 14:26.

4. "He who sent Me is true, and I speak to the world those things which I heard from Him" John 8:26.

5. "This is the work of God, that you believe in Him who He sent" John 6:29.

6. "Father into Your hands I commit My Spirit" Luke 23:46.

7. "My food is to do the will of Him who sent Me, and to finish His work" John 4:34.

8. "He who believes in Me, believes not in Me but in Him who sent Me" John 12:44.

9. "Most assuredly, I say to you, the Son can do nothing of Himself, but

what He sees the Father do, for whatever He does, the Son also does in like manner" John 5:19.

10. "The Spirit of the LORD is upon Me, Because He has anointed Me To preach the gospel to the poor" Luke 4:18.

11. "He who does not love Me does not keep My words, and the word which you hear is not Mine but the Father's who sent Me" John 14:24.

12. "For whoever does the will of God is My brother and My sister and mother" Mark   3:35.

13. "But that the world may know that I love the Father, and as the

Father gave Me commandment, so I do" John 14:31.

14. "Therefore, whatever I speak, just as the Father has told Me, so I speak" John:12:50.

15. "I proceeded forth and came from God, nor have I come of Myself, but He sent Me" John 8:42.

16. "My doctrine is not Mine, but His who sent Me" John 7:16.

17. "You will indeed drink My cup…But to sit on My right hand and My left hand is not Mine to give, but it is for those for whom it is prepared by My Father" John 8:40.

18. "All things have been delivered to Me by My Father" Matthew 11:27.

19. "As the living Father sent Me, and I live because of the Father, so he who feeds on Me will live because of Me" John 6:57.

NOTES & COMMENTS

NOTES & COMMENTS

NOTES & COMMENTS

NOTES & COMMENTS

NOTES & COMMENTS

NOTES & COMMENTS

www.ingramcontent.com/pod-product-compliance
Lightning Source LLC
Chambersburg PA
CBHW042125080426
42734CB00001B/5

9798218420741